The Everyday Slow Cooker Cookbook with 101 Amazing Breakfast and Dessert Recipes Inspired by the Medi...

by Vesela Tabakova

Text copyright(c)2016 Vesela Tabakova

Table Of Contents

Amazing Slow Cooker Family Dinners - Spend More Time Enjoying Your Meal And Less Time Preparing It!

We live in an age when everybody is constantly on the move and putting a home-cooked meal on the table during a busy weeknight is incredibly challenging. But no matter how hectic your day is, it is important that you take a moment and enjoy a good, hearty meal. Because while there may be more than one right way to eat, scientists agree on one thing – the more real, natural, unprocessed food you consume, the better.

While it may look and sound difficult to cook healthy food at home, after trying out some of my delicious slow cooker meals, you will soon realize you can produce a nutritious healthy dinner in no time. All my Mediterranean diet inspired recipes are super easy to throw together in the slow cooker in the morning. You just have to fill it up, plug it in, and come home to one of these cozy, comforting Mediterranean meals that will warm your soul and nourish your body!

Weeknight dinner ideas are hard to come by. For me, preparing delicious slow cooker meals is the easiest stress-free way of cooking healthy, yet amazingly tasty food for the family. My Mediterranean recipes use simple ingredients that you probably already have in your freezer, refrigerator, and pantry. They do not require complicated cooking techniques and are simply the best solution for fast-paced families who want tasty and healthy meals. At the end of a busy day a delicious slow cooked meal is the perfect answer to the question 'What's for dinner?'

Slow Cooker Soups

Mediterranean Chicken Soup

Serves 6-7

Ingredients:

about 2 lb chicken breasts

3-4 carrots, chopped

2 celery ribs, trimmed, halved, thinly sliced

1 red onion, chopped

1/3 cup rice

6 cups water

10 black olives, pitted and halved

1 bay leave

1/2 tsp salt

ground black pepper, to taste

lemon juice, to serve

fresh parsley or coriander, to serve

Directions:

Add all ingredients to the slow cooker and stir to combine. Cook on low for 6 to 8 hours, or until chicken is cooked and carrots and rice are tender.

Remove chicken from the slow cooker and let it cool slightly. Shred it and return it back to the soup. Serve soup with lemon juice and sprinkled with fresh parsley or coriander.

Moroccan Chicken and Butternut Squash Soup

Serves 5-6

Ingredients:

4 skinless, boneless chicken thighs, cut into bite-sized pieces

1 large onion, chopped

1 zucchini, quartered lengthwise and sliced into 1/2-inch pieces

3 cups peeled butternut squash, cut in 1/2-inch pieces

2 tbsp tomato paste diluted in 5 cups chicken broth

1/2 tsp ground cumin

1/4 tsp ground cinnamon

1 tsp paprika

1 tsp salt

4-5 basil leaves, chopped

1 tsp grated orange rind

Directions:

Place the chicken, vegetables and spices in the slow cooker. Pour the chicken broth over and stir to combine.

Cover and cook on low for 8-9 hours or until the chicken is cooked through and the squash is tender.

Slow Cooker French-style Farmhouse Chicken Soup

Serves 5-6

Ingredients:

4 skinless, boneless chicken thighs, cut into bite-sized pieces

1 leek, trimmed, halved, thinly sliced

1 celery rib, trimmed, halved, thinly sliced

2 carrots, chopped

1 fennel bulb, trimmed, diced

1 cup frozen peas

4 cups chicken broth

2 tbsp olive oil

1 tsp thyme

1 tsp salt

Directions:

Heat oil in a non-stick frying pan over medium-high heat. Add chicken and cook, turning, for 3-4 minutes or until browned all over. Transfer to slow cooker.

Add all other ingredients to the slow cooker. Pour the chicken broth over.

Cover and cook on low for 6-7 hours.

Chicken Vegetable Soup

Serves 6-7

Ingredients:

2 lb boneless chicken thighs, cut in bite sized pieces

1 small onion, chopped

1 celery rib, chopped

1/2 small parsnip, chopped

3 garlic cloves, chopped

1 carrot, chopped

1 red bell pepper, chopped

1 lb potatoes, peeled and cubed

5 cups chicken broth

1 tsp thyme

2 bay leaves

1 tsp salt

black pepper, to taste

1 tsp summer savory

Directions:

Season the chicken well with salt, ground black pepper and summer savory. Place it in a slow cooker with all remaining ingredients.

Cover and cook on low for 6-7 hours or on high for 4 hours.

Slow Cooker Chicken Noodle Soup

Serves 6-7

Ingredients:

2 lb boneless chicken thighs, cut in bite sized pieces

1 small onion, chopped

1 tomato, diced

1 red bell pepper, chopped

2-3 broccoli florets

4 cups chicken broth

2 cups wide egg noodles, uncooked

1 tsp garlic powder

1 tsp oregano

2 bay leaves

1 tsp salt

black pepper, to taste

Directions:

Season the chicken well with salt, black pepper garlic powder and oregano. Place it in a slow cooker with all remaining ingredients.

Cover and cook on low for 6-7 hours or on high for 4-5 hours.

Add noodles to slow cooker; cover and cook on low 20 minutes.

Bean, Chicken and Sausage Soup

Serves 4-5

Ingredients:

10.5 oz Italian sausage

2 bacon strips, diced

2 cups chicken, cooked and diced

1 can kidney beans, rinsed and drained

1 large onion, chopped

2 garlic cloves, crushed

4 cups water

1 can tomatoes, diced, undrained

1 bay leaf

1 tsp dried thyme

1 tsp summer savory

1/2 tsp dried basil

salt and pepper, to taste

Directions:

In a skillet, cook the sausage, onion and bacon over medium heat until the sausage is no longer pink. Drain off the fat. Add the garlic and cook for a minute more.

Add this mixture together with water, tomatoes and seasonings into the slow cooker. Cook on low for 6 hours. Add in the chicken and beans and cook for an hour more.

Easy Turkey Noodle Soup

Serves 6-7

Ingredients:

3 cups cooked leftover turkey, shredded or diced

1 small onion, chopped

2 carrots, sliced

5 cups chicken broth

8 ounces fettuccine noodles

1 tsp garlic powder

1 tsp oregano

2 bay leaves

1 tsp salt

black pepper, to taste

Directions:

Add the broth, turkey, carrots, onion, bay leaves, oregano, and pepper to the slow cooker.

Cover and cook on low for 8 hours or on high for 4-5 hours.

After the 8 hours are up, cook the noodles for about 10 minutes in boiling water on the stove top.

Add the drained noodles to the slow cooker with the soup, and continue to cook on high for about an 1 hour more.

Slow Cooker Chicken Broccoli Soup

Serves 6-7

Ingredients:

2 lb boneless chicken thighs, cut in bite sized pieces

1 small onion, chopped

1 fresh garlic clove

6-7 fresh or frozen broccoli florets

4 cups chicken broth

2 potatoes, peeled and cubed

3 tbsp olive oil

1 tsp garlic powder

1 tsp dried oregano

1 tsp salt

black pepper, to taste

12 oz cheddar cheese, to serve

Directions:

In a skillet, saute onion and garlic with olive oil until onion is translucent.

Season the chicken well with salt, black pepper, garlic powder and oregano. Place it in slow cooker with the onion mixture and all remaining ingredients.

Cover and cook on low for 8-10 hours or on high for 4-5 hours. Serve topped with cheddar cheese.

Slow Cooker Sausage, Spinach and Tomato Soup

Serves 4-5

Ingredients:

1 lb ground sweet Italian sausage

1 lb spinach, frozen

4 large carrots, chopped

1 can red beans

1 jar pasta sauce

1 small onion, finely cut

1-2 cloves garlic, crushed

1 carrot, chopped

3 cups vegetable broth

1 tbsp paprika

1 tsp dried mint

salt and black pepper, to taste

Directions:

Brown the sausage in a pan.

Add the sausage and all the other ingredients to the slow cooker and cook on low for 6-8 hours.

Slow Cooker Corn Chowder

Serves 4

Ingredients:

1 can whole kernel corn, undrained

1 small onion, finely chopped

2 potatoes, peeled and cubed

1 cup diced ham

1 celery stalk, chopped

3 cups vegetable broth

2 cups water

1 can evaporated milk

2-3 fresh coriander sprigs, to serve

Directions:

In a slow cooker, place the potatoes, onions, ham, celery, corn, salt and pepper to taste. Add vegetable broth.

Cook on low setting for 7-8 hours and then stir in the evaporated milk. Cook for 40 more minutes and serve topped with finely cut coriander leaves.

Italian Wedding Soup

Serves 4-5

Ingredients:

1 lb ground beef

1/3 cup breadcrumbs

1 egg, lightly beaten

1 onion, grated

2 carrots, chopped

1 small head escarole, trimmed and cut into 1/2-inch strips

1 cup baby spinach leaves

1 cup small pasta

3 cups chicken broth

2 cups water

2 tbsp Parmesan cheese, grated

2 tbsp fresh parsley, finely cut

3 tbsp olive oil

1 tsp dried oregano

1 tsp salt

1 tsp ground black pepper

Directions:

Combine ground beef, egg, onion, breadcrumbs, Parmesan cheese, parsley, 1/2 teaspoon of the salt and 1/2 teaspoon of the black pepper. Mix well with hands. Using a tablespoon, make walnut sized meatballs. Heat olive oil in a large skillet and brown meatballs in batches. Place aside on a plate.

Add broth, water, carrots, oregano, the remaining salt and pepper and the meatballs in a slow cooker. Cover and cook on low heat setting for about 8 hours.

Add in pasta, spinach and escarole and cook for an hour more.

Lentil and Beef Soup

Serves 5-6

Ingredients:

1 lb ground beef

1 cup dried brown or green lentils

2 carrots, chopped

1 onion, chopped

1 potato, cut into 1/2 inch cubes

4 garlic cloves, chopped

2 tomatoes, grated or pureed

3-4 cups water

1 tsp summer savory

1 tsp dried oregano

1 tsp paprika

2 tbsp olive oil

1 tsp salt

ground black pepper, to taste

Directions:

Heat olive oil in a skillet. Brown beef, breaking it up with a spoon. Add paprika and garlic and stir.

Combine all ingredients in crock pot. Cook on low for 11-12 hours or high for 6 hours.

Beef and Chickpea Soup

Serves 5-6

Ingredients:

2 slices bacon, chopped

1 cup ground beef

2 carrots, chopped

2 cloves garlic, finely chopped

1 large onion, chopped

1 celery rib, chopped

1 can tomatoes, chopped

3 cups beef broth

1 can chickpeas, drained

½ cup small pasta

1 bay leaf

1 tsp dried basil

1 tsp dried rosemary

1/4 tsp crushed chillies

Directions:

In a skillet, cook bacon and ground beef until well done, breaking up the beef as it cooks. Drain off the fat.

In a slow cooker, combine beef and bacon mixture, onion, carrots, celery, garlic, chillies, beef broth, tomatoes, and seasonings. Stir until all ingredients are combined. Cover, cook on low heat for 8-10 hours or on high for 5-6 hours.

About 1 hour before soup is done, stir in the chickpeas and pasta.

Italian Meatball Soup

Serves 5-6

Ingredients:

1 lb ground beef

1 small onion, grated

½ cup breadcrumbs

3-4 basil leaves, finely chopped

1 egg, lightly beaten

1 onion, chopped

2 garlic cloves, crushed

1 zucchini, diced

½ cup green beans, trimmed, halved

2 cups tomato sauce

3 cups water

½ cup small pasta

2 tbsp olive oil

salt and black pepper, to taste

1/3 cup Parmesan cheese, grated, to serve

Directions:

Combine ground beef, grated onion, garlic, breadcrumbs, basil, and egg in a large bowl. Season with salt and pepper. Mix well with hands and roll tablespoonfuls of the mixture into balls. Heat olive oil in a large skillet and brown meatballs in batches. Place aside on a plate.

Add water, tomato sauce, onion and the meatballs in a slow

cooker. Cover and cook on low for 9 hours.

About 1 hour before soup is done, stir in the zucchini, green beans and pasta.

Serve sprinkled with Parmesan cheese.

Bulgarian Beef Soup

Serves 5-6

Ingredients:

1.5 lbs beef shin, cut into large pieces

4 cups of water

3 carrots, peeled and cut into 3 inch pieces

2 onions, peeled and quartered

3-4 medium potatoes, peeled and quartered

1 celery rib, chopped

2 bay leaves

2 tsp salt

1 tsp black pepper

a bunch of fresh parsley, chopped, to serve

lemon juice, to serve

Directions:

Combine beef, onion, celery and water in a slow cooker. Add bay leaves, salt and black pepper.

Cover and cook on low for at least 12 hours or on high for 6-7 hours.

About 1 hour before soup is done, stir in the carrots and potatoes.

Serve with lemon juice and sprinkled with parsley.

Lamb Soup

Serves 5-6

Ingredients:

2 lbs lean boneless lamb, cubed

1 onion, finely cut

1 carrot, chopped

10 spring onions, chopped

2 tomatoes, diced

1/3 cup short-grained rice, rinsed

4 cups hot water

2 tbsp olive oil

1/2 tsp paprika

1 tsp salt

black pepper, to taste

1 tbsp dry mint

1/2 cup parsley, finely cut

Directions:

In a skillet, heat olive oil and gently brown the lamb. Add the meat together with all other ingredients into the slow cooker.

Stir, cover and cook on low for at least 12 hours or on high for 6-7 hours.

Hearty Lamb and Vegetable Soup

Serves 6-7

Ingredients:

2 cups roasted lamb, shredded

3 cups chicken or vegetable broth

1 cup water

1 cup canned tomatoes, diced, undrained

1 onion, chopped

1 large carrot, chopped

1 small turnip, chopped

1 celery rib

salt and black pepper, to taste

Directions:

Combine all ingredients in the slow cooker.

Cover and cook on low for 6-7 hours or on high for 4 hours. Season with salt and black pepper to taste and serve.

Creamy Zucchini Soup

Serves 4

Ingredients:

1 onion, finely chopped

2 garlic cloves, crushed

4 cups vegetable broth

5 zucchinis, peeled, thinly sliced

1 big potato, chopped

1/4 cup fresh basil leaves

1 tsp sugar

½ cup yogurt, to serve

Parmesan cheese, to serve

Directions:

Heat oil in a skillet over medium heat and sauté the onion and garlic, stirring, for 2-3 minutes or until soft.

Add the onion mixture together with the vegetable broth, water, zucchinis, potato and a teaspoon of sugar to a slow cooker. Cook on low for 6 hours or on high for 3 1/2 to 4 hours.

Season with salt and pepper, to taste. If you don't have an immersion blender, you can transfer the soup to a blender (in batches) and puree until smooth. Serve with a dollop of yogurt and/or sprinkled with Parmesan cheese.

Slow Cooker Tuscan-style Soup

Serves 5-6

Ingredients:

1 lb potatoes, peeled and cubed

1 small onion, chopped

1 can mixed beans, drained

1 carrot, chopped

2 garlic cloves, chopped

4 cups chicken broth

1 cups chopped kale

3 tbsp olive oil

1 bay leaf

salt and pepper, to taste

Parmesan cheese, to serve

Directions:

Heat oil in a skillet over medium heat and sauté the onion, carrot and garlic, stirring, for 2-3 minutes or until soft.

Combine all ingredients except the kale into the slow cooker. Season with salt and pepper to taste.

Cook on high for 4 hours or low for 6-7 hours. Add in kale about 30 minutes before soup is finished cooking. Serve sprinkled with Parmesan cheese.

Pumpkin and Bell Pepper Soup

Serves 4

Ingredients:

1 medium leek, chopped

3 cups pumpkin, peeled, deseeded, cut into small cubes

½ red pepper, chopped

1 can tomatoes, undrained

3 cups vegetable broth

½ tsp ground cumin

salt and black pepper, to taste

Directions:

Combine all ingredients in crock pot. Season with salt and pepper and cook on low for 6 hours. Blend in batches and cook 15 minutes more.

Moroccan Pumpkin Soup

Serves 6

Ingredients:

1 leek, white part only, thinly sliced

3 cloves garlic, finely chopped

2 carrots, peeled, coarsely chopped

2 lb pumpkin, peeled, deseeded, diced

1/3 cup chickpeas

4 cups vegetable broth

5 tbsp olive oil

juice of ½ lemon

½ tsp ground ginger

½ tsp ground cinnamon

½ tsp ground cumin

salt and pepper, to taste

1/2 cup chopped parsley, to serve

Directions:

Heat olive oil in a skillet and gently sauté leek and garlic until soft. Add in cinnamon, ginger and cumin and stir.

Add this mixture to the slow cooker together with carrots, pumpkin and chickpeas. Add vegetable broth and salt and pepper.

Cover and cook on low 6 hours. Blend in batches and return to slow cooker. Cook for 10 minutes more. Serve topped with parsley

Spinach, Leek and Quinoa Soup

Serves 5-6

Ingredients:

½ cup uncooked quinoa, rinsed well

2 leeks halved lengthwise and sliced

1 onion, chopped

2 garlic cloves, chopped

1 tbsp olive oil

1 can of diced tomatoes, undrained

2 cups fresh spinach, chopped

3 cups vegetable broth

salt and pepper, to taste

Directions:

Heat a skillet over medium heat. Add olive oil and onion and sauté for 2 minutes. Add in leeks and cook for another 2-3 minutes, then add garlic and stir.

Add sautéed vegetables and all remaining ingredients except the spinach into the slow cooker. Season with salt and pepper to taste. Cook on high for 4 hours or low for 6-7 hours. Add spinach about 30 minutes before soup is finished cooking.

Quinoa, White Bean, and Kale Soup

Serves 5-6

Ingredients:

½ cup uncooked quinoa, rinsed well

1 small onion, chopped

1 can diced tomatoes, undrained

2 cans cannellini beans, undrained

3 cups chopped kale

2 garlic cloves, chopped

4 cups vegetable broth

1 tsp paprika

1 tsp dried mint

salt and pepper, to taste

Directions:

Combine all ingredients except the kale into the slow cooker. Season with salt and pepper to taste.

Cook on high for 4 hours or low for 6-7 hours. Add in kale about 30 minutes before soup is finished cooking.

Mediterranean Chickpea Soup

Serves 5-6

Ingredients:

1 can chickpeas, drained

a bunch of spring onions, finely cut

2 cloves garlic, crushed

1 can tomatoes, diced

4 cups vegetable broth

1/2 medium cabbage, cored and cut into 8 wedges

3 tbsp olive oil

1 bay leaf

½ tsp rosemary

½ cup freshly grated Parmesan cheese

Directions:

In a skillet, gently sauté onion and garlic in olive oil. Add to the slow cooker together with broth, chickpeas, tomatoes, bay leaf and rosemary.

Cook on high setting for 4 hours. Nestle cabbage into the soup, cover and cook until it is tender, about 20 minutes on high. Serve sprinkled with Parmesan cheese.

French Vegetable Soup

Serves 4-5

Ingredients:

1 leek, thinly sliced

1 large zucchini, peeled and diced

1 cup green beans, halved

2 large potatoes, peeled and cut into large chunks

1 medium fennel bulb, trimmed, cored, and cut into large chunks

2 garlic cloves, cut

4 cups vegetable broth

black pepper, to taste

4 tbsp freshly grated Parmesan cheese

Directions:

Combine all ingredients in slow cooker. Season with salt and pepper to taste. Cook on low for 6-10 hours or high for 2.5-3 hours.

Serve warm sprinkled with Parmesan cheese.

Moroccan Lentil Soup

Serves 8-9

Ingredients:

1 cup red lentils

1/2 cup canned chickpeas, drained

2 onions, chopped

2 cloves garlic, minced

1 cup canned tomatoes, chopped

1/2 cup canned white beans, drained

3 carrots, diced

3 celery ribs, diced

6 cups water

1 tsp ginger, grated

1 tsp ground cardamom

Directions:

Add all ingredients into slow cooker. Cover and cook on low for 8 hours or high for 4 hours.

Season with salt to taste and puree half the soup in a food processor or blender.

Return the pureed soup to the slow cooker, stir and serve.

Heartwarming Split Pea Soup

Serves 5-6

Ingredients:

1 lb dried green split peas, rinsed and drained

2 potatoes, peeled and diced

1 small onion, chopped

1 celery rib, chopped

1 carrot, chopped

2 garlic cloves, chopped

1 bay leaf

1 tsp black pepper

1/2 tsp salt

6 cups water

Grated feta cheese, to serve

Directions:

Combine all ingredients in slow cooker.

Cover and cook on low for 5-6 hours.

Discard bay leaf. Blend soup to desired consistency, adding additional hot water to thin, if desired.

Sprinkle grated feta cheese on top and serve with garlic or herb bread.

Minestrone

Serves 4-5

Ingredients:

¼ cabbage, chopped

2 carrots, chopped

1 celery rib, thinly sliced

1 small onion, chopped

2 garlic cloves, chopped

4 cups vegetable broth

1 cup canned tomatoes, diced, undrained

1 cup fresh spinach, torn

black pepper and salt, to taste

Directions:

Add all ingredients except spinach into slow cooker. Cover and cook on low for 6-7 hours or high for 4 hours.

Add spinach about 30 minutes before soup is finished cooking.

Slow Cooker Summer Garden Soup

Serves 4-5

Ingredients:

1 small onion, finely cut

2 carrots, chopped

1 zucchini, peeled and cubed

1 box frozen baby lima beans, thawed

1 celery rib, thinly sliced

2 garlic cloves, chopped

4 cups vegetable broth

1 can tomatoes, diced, undrained

1 medium yellow summer squash, cubed

1 cup uncooked small pasta

3-4 tbsp pesto

black pepper and salt, to taste

Directions:

Add all ingredients except zucchini, summer squash and pasta into slow cooker. Cover and cook on low for 6 hours or high for 4 hours.

Stir in pasta, zucchini and yellow squash. Cover; cook 1 hour longer or until vegetables are tender. Top individual servings with pesto.

Crock Pot Tomato Basil Soup

Serves: 5-6

Ingredients:

4 cups chopped fresh tomatoes or 27 oz can tomatoes

1/3 cup rice

3 cups water

1 large onion, diced

4 garlic cloves, minced

3 tbsp olive oil

1 tsp salt

1 tbsp dried basil

1 tbsp paprika

1 tsp sugar

½ bunch fresh parsley, to serve

Directions:

In a skillet, sauté onion and garlic for 2-3 minutes. When onions have softened, add them together with all other ingredients to the crock pot.

Cook on low for 5-7 hours, or on high for 3 1/2. Blend with an immersion blender and serve topped with fresh parsley.

Cheesy Cauliflower Soup

Serves 4-5

Ingredients:

1 large onion, finely cut

1 medium head cauliflower, chopped

2-3 garlic cloves, minced

4 cups vegetable broth

1 cup whole cream

1 cup cheddar cheese, grated

salt, to taste

fresh ground black pepper, to taste

Directions:

Put cauliflower, onion, garlic and vegetable broth in crock pot. Cover and cook on low for 4-6 hours. Blend in a blender.

Return to crock pot and blend in cream and cheese. Season with salt and pepper and stir to mix.

Creamy Artichoke Soup

Serves 4

Ingredients:

1 can artichoke hearts, drained

3 potatoes, peeled and cut into ½-inch pieces

1 small onion, finely cut

2 cloves garlic, crushed

3 cups vegetable broth

2 tbsp lemon juice

1 cup heavy cream

black pepper, to taste

Directions:

Combine the potatoes, onion, artichoke hearts, broth, lemon juice and black pepper in the slow cooker.

Cover and cook on low for 8-10 hours or on high for 4-5 hours or until the potatoes are tender.

Blend the soup in batches and return it to the slow cooker. Add the cream and continue to cook

until heated 5-10 minutes more. Garnish with a swirl of cream or a sliver of artichoke.

Tomato Artichoke Soup

Serves 4

Ingredients:

1 can artichoke hearts, drained

1 can diced tomatoes, undrained

3 cups vegetable broth

1 small onion, chopped

2 cloves garlic, crushed

1 tbsp pesto

black pepper, to taste

Directions:

Combine all ingredients in the slow cooker.

Cover and cook on low for 8-10 hours or on high for 4-5 hours.

Blend the soup in batches and return it to the slow cooker. Season with salt and pepper to taste and serve.

Slow Cooker Main Dishes

Mediterranean Chicken Stew

Serves 4

Ingredients:

4 chicken breast halves

1 large onion, sliced

1 red bell pepper, thinly sliced

2 cups tomato pasta sauce

1/2 cup black olives, pitted

1/2 green olives, pitted

1/3 cup Parmesan cheese

¼ cup chopped parsley

Directions:

Spray the slow cooker with non stick spray.

Combine all ingredients into slow cooker and turn chicken to coat. Cook on low for 7-8 hours.

Sprinkle with Parmesan cheese, parsley and serve.

Slow Cooker Herb Chicken and Vegetables

Serves 4

Ingredients:

4 skinless, boneless chicken breast halves

12 oz baby potatoes

1 onion, sliced

2 carrots, cut

1 red bell pepper, halved, deseeded, cut

1 zucchini, peeled and cut

4 garlic cloves, thinly sliced

1 cup chicken broth

1 tsp dry oregano

1 tsp dried rosemary

salt and pepper, to taste

Directions:

Spray the slow cooker with non stick spray.

Place vegetables in slow cooker. Season with a bit of salt and pepper.

Season chicken breasts with oregano and rosemary and place on top of vegetables.

Pour chicken broth over the chicken and vegetables. Cover and cook on low for about 6-7 hours.

Chicken and Onion Crock Pot

Serves 4

Ingredients:

4 chicken breast halves

4-5 big onions, thinly sliced

1/2 cup black olives, pitted

4 tbsp olive oil

1 tsp thyme

1 tsp tumeric

salt and black pepper, to taste

1/4 cup parsley leaves, chopped, to serve

Directions:

Heat the oil in a large, deep frying pan over medium-high heat. Season chicken breasts with thyme and tumeric and cook it, turning, for 4-5 minutes or until golden. Transfer to slow cooker.

Place onions and olives on top of chicken. Add chicken broth, cover, and cook on low for about 6-7 hours.

Crock Pot Mediterranean Chicken Drumsticks

Serves 4

Ingredients:

8 chicken drumsticks

1 leek, trimmed, thinly sliced

2 garlic cloves, crushed

1 can tomatoes

1 can chickpeas, drained and rinsed

1 tsp dry rosemary

1 tsp paprika

salt and pepper, to taste

Directions:

Spray the slow cooker with non stick spray.

Place all ingredients into slow cooker and turn drumsticks to coat well.

Cook on low for 5-6 hours.

Serve with cooked orzo or couscous.

Crock Pot Chicken and Leek Drumsticks

Serves 4

Ingredients:

8 chicken drumsticks

4-5 leeks, trimmed, thinly sliced

4-5 white button mushrooms, sliced

2 garlic cloves, crushed

1/2 cup dry white wine

1 cup frozen peas

1 cup heavy cream

1 tbsp chopped fresh taragon

salt and pepper, to taste

Directions:

Spray the slow cooker with non stick spray.

Place all ingredients into slow cooker and turn drumsticks to coat well.

Cook on low for 6-7 hours.

Slow Cooker Greek Chicken Stew

Serves 4

Ingredients:

4 skinless, boneless chicken breast halves or 8 tights

1 lb potatoes, peeled and cubed

1 lb green beans, trimmed and cut in 1 inch pieces

1 large onion, chopped

5 cloves garlic, minced

1 can tomatoes, undrained

1/2 cup feta cheese, crumbled

salt and black pepper, to taste

Directions:

Spray the slow cooker with non stick spray.

Place all ingredients into slow cooker and turn chicken breasts to coat well.

Cook on low setting for 6-7 hours and then stir in the feta cheese. Cook for 40 more minutes and serve.

Whole Chicken with Sumac

1 whole chicken (3-4 lbs)

2 tbsp olive oil

2 garlic cloves, crushed

1 tbsp sumac

1 tsp lemon zest

1 tbsp lemon juice

salt and black pepper, to taste

Directions:

Combine olive oil, garlic, sumac, lemon rind, lemon juice, salt and pepper in a bowl. Rub mixture over chicken. Cover and marinate for 2 hours if time permits.

Cook in slow cooker on low until no longer pink at the bone and the juices run clear, 6 to 8 hours.

Chicken with Almonds and Prunes

Serves 4

Ingredients:

2 lbs chicken thigh fillets, trimmed

1/2 cup fresh orange juice

2 tbsp honey

1/3 cup white wine

1/2 cup pitted prunes

2 tbsp blanched almonds

2 tbsp raisins or sultanas

1 tsp ground cinnamon

salt and ground black pepper, to taste

1 tbsp fresh parsley leaves, chopped

Directions:

Spray the slow cooker with non stick spray.

Place all ingredients into slow cooker and turn chicken fillets to coat well.

Cook on low for 6-7 hours.

Slow Cooked Moroccan Chicken Tagine

Serves 4-5

Ingredients:

1 whole chicken (3-4 lbs), cut into pieces

2 large onions, grated

2 or 3 cloves of garlic, finely chopped or pressed

1 tsp ginger

1 tsp cumin

1 tsp paprika

1 tsp black pepper

1 tsp tumeric

1/2 teaspoon salt

1/2 cup green or black olives, or mixed

1-2 preserved lemons, quartered and deseeded

5 tbsp olive oil

one bunch of fresh coriander

one bunch fresh parsley leaves

Directions:

Rinse and dry chicken and place onto a clean plate.

In a large bowl, mix three tablespoons of olive oil, salt, half the onions, garlic, ginger, cumin, paprika, and tumeric. Mix thoroughly, crush the garlic with your fingers, and add a little water to make a paste.

Roll the chicken pieces into the marinade and leave for 10 to 15 minutes.

In a slow cooker, add the chicken and pour excess marinade juices over the top. Add the remaining onions, olives and chopped preserved lemon. Tie the parsley and coriander together into a bouquet and place on top of the chicken.

Cover and cook on low for 6-7 hours. Remove the parsley bouquet and serve over cooked rice or couscous.

Slow Cooker Chicken Moussaka

Serves 6

Ingredients:

2 big eggplants, cut into 1/2 inch thick rounds

olive oil cooking spray

1 tbsp salt

1 large onion, finely cut

1/2 tsp ground cinnamon

1/2 tsp ground nutmeg

1/4 tsp ground coriander

1/4 tsp ground ginger

2 cups canned tomatoes, undrained, chopped

2 cups skinless, shredded, roast chicken

1/2 cup finely chopped fresh parsley leaves

1 tsp sugar

for the topping:

1 cup yogurt

3 eggs

1 cup Parmesan cheese

salt and black pepper, to taste

Directions:

Place eggplant slices on a tray and sprinkle with plenty of salt.
Let sit for 30 minutes, then rinse with cold water. Lay slices out
flat and use a clean kitchen towel to squeeze out excess water and

pat dry.

Heat a frying pan over medium high heat. Spray both sides of eggplant with oil. Cook in batches for 3 to 4 minutes each side or until golden. Transfer to a plate.

In the same pan sauté onion, stirring, for 3 to 4 minutes or until softened. Add spice. Sauté for one minute until fragrant. Add tomatoes and sugar, stir and sauté until thickened. Add chicken and parsley and stir well to combine.

Arrange half the eggplant slices in the slow cooker. Cover with chicken and tomato mixture and arrange remaining eggplant.

Cover the slow cooker, and cook on high heat for 2 hours.

Mix the eggs, yogurt, Parmesan and put over the top of eggplant using a spoon. Replace the lid and cook on low heat for 1 to 1½ hours.

Portuguese Style Chicken

Serves 4

Ingredients:

1 whole chicken

4 garlic cloves, crushed

1/3 cup lime juice

3 tbsp olive oil

1 tbsp chilli flakes

1 tsp ground coriander

1 tbsp paprika

1 tsp dried oregano

1 tsp salt

Directions:

Using a sharp knife, cut through bones on either side of backbone. Remove backbone, place chicken breast side up into a bowl.

Combine lime juice, olive oil, garlic, chilli, salt, coriander, paprika and oregano together in a cup. Pour over chicken, cover, and refrigerate for at least two hours.

In a slow cooker, add the chicken and pour excess marinade juices over the top. Cook on low for 6-7 hours. Serve with vegetable salad or boiled potatoes.

Slow Cooked Chicken with Tomatoes and Artichokes

Serves 4

Ingredients:

3 skinless chicken breasts, cut into strips

2 leeks, white parts only, chopped

1 can quartered artichokes, drained

1 can diced tomatoes

1/2 green olives, halved

2 garlic cloves, crushed

1 tsp lemon rind

7-8 fresh basil leaves, chopped

1 bay leaf

salt and pepper, to taste

1 cup finely cut parsley

Directions:

Spray the slow cooker with non stick spray.

Combine all ingredients into slow cooker and turn chicken to coat. Cook on low for 7-8 hours. Remove bay leave and serve sprinkled with parsley.

Easy Chicken Parmigiana

Serves 4

Ingredients:

4 chicken breast fillets

1 eggplant, peeled and sliced lengthwise

1 can tomatoes, diced and undrained

9 oz mozzarella cheese, sliced

1 tsp dried basil

salt and pepper, to taste

Directions:

Spray the slow cooker with non stick spray.

Combine all ingredients except the mozzarella cheese into slow cooker and turn chicken to coat. Cook on low for 5 hours or high 4-6 hours.

Add the mozzarella and continue to cook until heated 25 minutes more.

Slow Cooker Mediterranean Turkey

Serves 4

Ingredients:

1 boneless turkey breast, trimmed

1 large red onion, sliced

2-3 garlic cloves, chopped

1/3 cup dry white wine

1/2 cup chicken broth

1 cup black olives, pitted

1 tbsp dried thyme

1 cup oil-packed sun-dried tomatoes

salt and black pepper, to taste

Directions:

Combine all ingredients in slow cooker. Cover and cook on low 7-8 hours. Cut turkey into slices and serve.

Mediterranean Seafood Stew

Serves 4

Ingredients:

1 ½ flounder or sole fillets

3/4 pound shelled uncooked medium shrimp, tails removed

3 tomatoes, chopped

1 onion, chopped

2 cloves garlic, chopped

1/3 cup white wine

20 black olives, pitted and chopped

1 tbsp capers

1 tbsp fresh lemon juice

1 tsp dried oregano

4 leaves fresh basil, chopped

3 tbsp Parmesan cheese

Directions:

Spray a slow cooker with non stick spray. Place the shrimp, onion, garlic, oregano, tomatoes, wine, olives, capers, lemon juice and chopped basil in it. Cook on high for 4 hours, then add in fish and cook for an additional 30-45 minutes or until fish is flaky.

Serve sprinkled with Parmesan cheese.

Slow Cooker Mediterranean Salmon

Serves 4

Ingredients:

1 lb salmon fillets

2 tomatoes, chopped

1 onion, chopped

1 red bell pepper, chopped

1 zucchini, peeled and sliced

1 tbsp capers

1 tbsp fresh lemon juice

1 tsp garlic powder

1 tsp dried dill

1/2 tsp black pepper

1 tsp salt

Directions:

Wrap all ingredients in aluminum foil and then place inside the slow cooker.

Cook on low for 6 hours or until salmon is cooked through and flakes easily.

Slow Cooked Lamb with Red Wine Sauce

Serves 4

Ingredients:

4 trimmed lamb shanks

1 onion, thinly sliced

2 large carrots, roughly chopped

2-3 parsnips, roughly chopped

1 cup chicken broth

2 cups dry red wine

1 tsp brown sugar

½ tsp black pepper

½ tsp salt

Directions:

Spray the slow cooker with non stick spray.

Place the lamb shanks in it together with all other ingredients.

Cover and cook on low for 6-7 hours.

Slow Cooked Mediterranean Lamb

Serves 4

Ingredients:

1 1/2 lb boneless leg of lamb, trimmed and cubed

1 onion, thinly sliced

2 large carrots, roughly chopped

2 garlic cloves, chopped

1 cup chicken broth

1 can chickpeas, drained

1 cup raisins

1/2 cup dried figs, halved

4 tbsp fresh mint, finely cut

1/4 tsp saffron threads, crushed

1 tsp ground ginger

½ tsp black pepper

½ tsp salt

3 tbsp olive oil

Directions:

Heat oil in a large non stick frying pan and cook the lamb in batches, for 3-4 minutes each side, or until golden. Transfer to slow cooker.

Add in all other ingredients. Cover and cook on low for 7-9 hours.

Slow Cooked Lamb with Lemon, Dill and Feta

Serves 4

Ingredients:

4 lamb shanks

1 small onion, thinly sliced

2 garlic cloves, chopped

1 cup chicken broth

1/2 cup fresh dill, finely cut

1 medium lemon, thinly sliced

1 cup crumbled feta cheese

2 tbsp olive oil

½ tsp black pepper

½ tsp salt

3 tbsp olive oil

Directions:

Season the lamb shanks with salt and pepper. Heat oil in a large non stick frying pan and cook the lamb in batches, for 3-4 minutes each side, or until golden. Transfer to slow cooker.

Add the chicken broth, 2 tablespoons of dill, garlic, onion and lemon slices. Cover and cook on low until the lamb is tender, about 8-9 hours.

Sprinkle with the feta and the remaining dill and serve with orzo or rice.

Slow Cooked Lamb and Apricot Couscous

Serves 4

Ingredients:

1 lb stewing lamb pieces

1 onion, thinly sliced

2 cups bag baby carrots

6-7 dried apricots

1 garlic clove, chopped

1 cup chicken broth

1/2 cup raisins

4 tbsp fresh mint, finely cut

1/4 tsp saffron threads, crushed

1 tsp ground ginger

½ tsp black pepper

½ tsp salt

3 tbsp olive oil

1/2 cup coriander leaves, finely cut, to serve

lemon wedges, to serve

Directions:

Heat oil in a large non stick frying pan and cook the lamb in batches, for 3-4 minutes each side, or until golden. Transfer to slow cooker.

Add in all other ingredients. Cover and cook on low for 7-9 hours.

Serve with couscous, mint or coriander leaves, and lemon wedges.

Easy Lamb and Butternut Squash Tagine

Serves 4

Ingredients:

1 lb stewing lamb pieces

1 small onion, finely cut

2 carrots, chopped

1 small butternut squash, peeled, seeds removed and diced

1 garlic clove, chopped

1 cup chicken broth

1 tbsp honey

1/4 tsp saffron threads, crushed

1 tsp ground ginger

½ tsp black pepper

½ tsp salt

3 tbsp olive oil

1/2 cup chopped coriander, to serve

4 tbsp toasted pine nuts, to serve

Directions:

Heat oil in a large non stick frying pan and cook the lamb in batches, for 3-4 minutes each side, or until golden. Transfer to slow cooker.

Add in all other ingredients. Cover and cook on low for 7-9 hours.

Serve with couscous, coriander leaves, and toasted pine nuts.

Lamb, Spinach and Chickpea Stew

Serves 4

Ingredients:

1 lb stewing lamb pieces

1 small onion, finely cut

2 carrots, chopped

1 tomato, diced

2 cups spinach, chopped

1 can chickpeas, drained

1 garlic clove, chopped

1 cup chicken broth

1 tbsp paprika

½ tsp black pepper

½ tsp salt

3 tbsp olive oil

1 cup yogurt, to serve

Directions:

Heat oil in a large non stick frying pan and cook the lamb in batches, for 3-4 minutes each side, or until golden. Transfer to slow cooker.

Add in all other ingredients except the spinach. Cover and cook on low for 6-7 hours. Add in the spinach, cover and cook on high until the spinach is wilted, about 10 minutes.

Serve with a dollop of yogurt.

Ground Beef, Quinoa and Brussels Sprouts

Serves: 4

Ingredients:

6 oz ground beef

1/2 small onion, finely cut

2 garlic cloves, crushed

1 cup quinoa

2 cups chicken broth

1 large sweet potato, peeled and grated

1 cup grated Brussels sprouts

1 tbsp olive oil

Directions:

Spray the slow cooker with non stick spray.

In a saucepan, heat the olive oil over medium heat. Gently saute the onion and garlic until fragrant. Add in the ground beef, breaking it up as it cooks.

Combine quinoa and chicken broth in a slow cooker. Add in ground beef mixture and all other ingredients.

Cover and cook on high for 2 hours.

Italian Beef Stew

Serves 4

Ingredients:

1.5 lbs stewing beef

3 carrots, cut

1 medium onion, sliced

3 garlic cloves, chopped

1 can white beans, drained

1/2 cup beef broth

1 can diced tomatoes, undrained

2 cups frozen green beans

2/3 cup fresh basil leaves, chopped

1 tsp sugar

Directions:

Spray the slow cooker with non stick spray.

Place beef, carrots, onion, garlic, beans, tomatoes and beef broth in slow cooker.

Cover and cook on low for 10-11 hours.

Stir in basil, sugar and frozen green beans. Increase heat setting to high, cover and cook 30 minutes or until green beans are tender.

Beef Stew with Quince

Serves 6-8

Ingredients:

2 lbs chuck roast, trimmed of fat and cut into 2 inch pieces

2 onions, chopped

2-3 tomatoes, pureed

1-2 bay leaves

1 cinnamon stick

1 cup dry white wine

3 quinces, peeled, cored and cubed

5-6 prunes

1 tsp paprika

1 tsp salt

1/2 tsp black pepper

1 tbsp honey

3 tbsp olive oil

Directions:

Heat the olive oil in a large pot over medium-high heat. Seal the meat in batches, then set it aside in slow cooker.

Add in all other ingredients, cover, and cook on low for 11-12 hours. Discard cinnamon stick and bay leaves and serve.

Slow Cooked Beef Couscous

Serves 5-6

Ingredients:

2 lbs stewing beef

1 large onion, cut

1/2 cup canned chickpeas, drained

2 carrots

1/2 cup green peas

1/2 cup black olives, pitted

3 tbsp tomato paste

2 beef broth

1 zucchini, peeled and cut

1 cup frozen green beans

3 potatoes, peeled and cut

1 tsp cumin

1 tsp paprika

a small bunch of fresh parsley

Directions:

Place beef, onion, chickpeas, green peas, carrot, olives, tomato paste, cumin, paprika and beef broth in slow cooker. Tie the parsley into a bouquet and place it on top.

Cover and cook on low for 10 hours. Add green beans, potatoes and zucchini, season with salt and pepper to taste, increase heat setting to high and cook for 1 hour more. In the end discard the parsley bouquet.

Serve over cooked couscous with meat and vegetables on top and stew sauce in a separate bowl.

Easy Beef Crock Pot

Serves 4

Ingredients:

2 lbs beef, cubed

1 small onion, finely cut

1 celery rib, finely cut

1 can cream of mushrooms soup

½ cup water or vegetable broth

Directions:

Spray the slow cooker with non stick spray.

Combine all ingredients into the slow cooker, cover, and cook on low for 7-9 hours.

Beef and Pumpkin Stew

Serves 4-5

Ingredients:

2 lbs lean beef, cubed

2 cups cubed pumpkin

1 small onion, chopped

2 garlic cloves, chopped

1 tomato, diced

zest of one orange

1 bay leaf

1 tsp paprika

4 tbsp olive oil

salt and black pepper, to taste

3 green onions, chopped, to serve

Directions:

Spray the slow cooker with non stick spray.

Combine all ingredients into the slow cooker, cover, and cook on low for 7-9 hours.

Sprinkle with green onions and serve.

Beef and Root Vegetable Crock Pot

Serves 6

Ingredients:

2 lbs stewing beef

2 carrots, cut

2 onions, sliced

1 small turnip, peeled and diced

1 small beet, peeled and diced

1 cup beef broth

1 tsp tomato paste

1 tbsp paprika

2 bay leaves

1 cup yogurt, to serve

Directions:

Spray the crock pot with non stick spray.

Combine all ingredients in crock pot. Cover and cook on low for 6-9 hours.

Beef and Chickpea Crock Pot

Serves 4

Ingredients:

2 lbs lean beef meat, cubed

2 onions, chopped

1 can chickpeas, drained

1 red bell pepper, chopped

1 tbsp tomato paste

1 cup beef broth

1 tsp paprika

1 tsp cumin

salt, to taste

Directions:

Combine all ingredients in crock pot. Cover and cook for 6-7 hours on low or 4 hours on high heat.

Cabbage and Beef Stew

Serves 6-8

Ingredients:

3 2-inch center cut beef shanks

1 medium cabbage, cut into thin strips

1 onion, chopped

1 carrot, chopped

1 red bell pepper, cut into strips

2 tomatoes, chopped

1 tsp paprika

1/2 tsp cumin

1/2 tsp cinnamon

1 cup chicken broth

salt, to taste

1 1/2 cups water

Directions:

Combine cabbage, onion, carrot, pepper and tomatoes in slow cooker. Season with salt and pepper to taste, add in paprika, cumin and cinnamon. Place the beef shanks on top of the vegetables and add in the chicken broth.

Cover and cook on low heat for 9 hours. Remove and shred the meat and serve.

Mixed Vegetables with Beef

Serves 6-8

Ingredients:

2 lbs stewing beef

2 eggplants, peeled and cubed

5 small potatoes, halved

1 zucchini, peeled and cubed

2 red peppers, cut

1 cup frozen okra

1 cup frozen peas

1 cup frozen green beans

1 onion, sliced

4 garlic cloves, cut

3 tomatoes, diced

4 tbsp olive oil

1 tsp paprika

salt, to taste

black pepper, to taste

1 cup parsley leaves, chopped

Directions:

Sprinkle the eggplant pieces with salt and set aside in a strainer
for 15 minutes. Wash the salt and the excess juices and pat dry the
eggplant pieces.

minutes until well browned. Transfer to crock pot. Add in eggplants, onion, garlic, peas, green beans, tomatoes, okra and red peppers. Stir in chicken broth and paprika. Season with salt and pepper to taste. cover and cook on low heat for 6-7 hours.

Two hours before the stew is done, add in the zucchini and potatoes.

Serve sprinkled with parsley.

Ground Beef and Rice Stuffed Peppers

Serves 6

Ingredients:

8-9 red or green bell peppers, cored and seeded

2 lbs ground beef

1/4 cup rice, washed and drained

1 onion, finely cut

1 tomato, grated

a bunch of fresh parsley, chopped

1 cup warm water

3 tbsp olive oil

1 tbsp paprika

salt and pepper, to taste

Directions:

Heat the oil and sauté the onion for 2-3 minutes. Remove from heat. Add in paprika, ground beef, rice, tomato, and parsley and season with salt and pepper. Combine very well and stuff each pepper with the mixture using a spoon. Every pepper should be 3/4 full.

Arrange the peppers in slow cooker and top up with warm water. Cover and cook for about 7 hours on low heat. Serve with yogurt.

Stuffed Tomatoes with Bulgur and Ground Beef

Serves 6

Ingredients:

1 lb ground beef

6 large tomatoes

2 tbsp tomato paste or purée

1/2 cup bulgur

1 onion, shredded

2 garlic cloves, crushed

6 tsp sugar

1 tsp paprika

1 tsp mint

1/2 cup parsley leaves, finely cut

1 cup chicken broth

5 tbsp olive oil

salt and pepper, to taste

Directions:

Slice the tops of the tomatoes in such a way as to be able to stuff the tomato and cover with the cap. With the help of a spoon, scoop out the tomato flesh and reserve in a bowl. Sprinkle a tsp of sugar in each tomato to help reduce the acidity.

Heat the olive oil in a large skillet and brown the ground beef. Add the onions and garlic and cook until transparent. Add the bulgur, parsley, finely cut tomato pulp and tomato paste. Season with paprika, mint, salt and pepper. Bring to the boil then reduce heat and simmer for 5 minutes.

Arrange the tomatoes in the slow cooker. Stuff them with the meat mixture - each tomato should be about 3/4 full. Add chicken broth, cover, and cook for 6 hours on low heat.

Stuffed Cabbage Leaves with Ground Beef and Rice

Serves 8

Ingredients:

1 lb ground beef

20-30 medium sized pickled cabbage leaves

1 onion, diced

1 leek, finely cut

1/2 cup white rice

2 tsp tomato paste

2 tbsp olive oil

2 tsp paprika

1/2 tsp cumin

1 tsp dried mint

½ tsp black pepper

salt, to taste

Directions:

Sauté the onion and leek in the oil for about 2-3 minutes. Remove from heat and add the beef, tomato paste, paprika, mint, cumin, black pepper and the washed and drained rice. Add salt only if the cabbage leaves are not too salty. Mix everything very well.

Place a cabbage leaf on a large plate with the thickest part closest to you. Spoon 1-2 teaspoons of the meat mixture and fold over each edge to create a tight sausage-like parcel. Place in the slow cooker in two or three layers.

Cover with a few cabbage leaves and pour over some boiling water so that the water level remains lower than the top layer of cabbage leaves.

Cover and cook on low heat for 6-9 hours.

Meatballs in Tomato Sauce

Serves 6

Ingredients:

2 lbs ground beef

2 onions, grated

1 cup breadcrumbs

1 egg, beaten

1/3 cup parsley leaves, finely chopped, for the meatballs

1 carrot, chopped

2 garlic cloves, cut

3-4 white button mushrooms, sliced

1 red pepper, cut

1 can tomatoes, diced and undrained

1/2 cup chicken broth

1/2 cup parsley leaves, to serve

Directions:

In a bowl, mix the ground beef, breadcrumbs, parsley, onion, and egg. Shape the mixture into meatballs.

In a slow cooker, mix the tomato sauce with the vegetables. Place the meatballs into the sauce mixture. Cook on Low for 6-8 hours.

Meatloaf with Vegetables

Serves 6-8

Ingredients:

2 lbs ground beef

2 eggs, lightly beaten

4 large potatoes, cut

5-6 zucchinis, cut

5-6 tomatoes, cut

1 cup chicken broth

3 tbsp olive oil

1/2 cup fresh parsley, finely cut

2 tsp of salt

1 tsp black pepper

1/2 tsp salt

Directions:

Combine ground beef, eggs, olive oil, parsley, salt, and pepper in a bowl and mix with hands. Make a loaf and arrange it in the center of a slow cooker.

Peel and cut potatoes and zucchinis. Puree tomatoes. Arrange vegetables around the meatloaf, season with salt, add chicken broth and stir. Cook on low for 3-4 hours. Remove meatloaf from slow cooker to serving platter. Cut into pieces and serve with vegetables.

Mediterranean Meatloaf

Serves 4

Ingredients:

1 lb ground beef

1/3 cup brown rice

1 small red onion, grated

1 carrot, peeled, grated

3 oz feta cheese, crumbled

2 tbsp tomato sauce

1 egg, lightly beaten

2 tbsp basil leaves, finely cut

1 zucchini, thinly sliced

1 cup cherry tomatoes

1 garlic clove, crushed

2-3 tbsp olive oil

Directions:

Cook rice following package directions. Set aside to cool.

Combine rice, onion, ground beef, carrot, feta, sauce, egg and basil in a bowl. Shape mixture into loaf, and place in center of slow cooker. Place zucchini, tomatoes and garlic in a bowl. Toss in olive oil. Arrange over meatloaf.

Cover and cook on low for 3-4 hours. Remove meatloaf from slow cooker to serving platter. Cut into pieces to serve.

Potato Moussaka

Serves 4

Ingredients:

1 lb ground beef

1 celery rib, finely chopped

1 carrot, peeled, finely chopped

1 onion, finely chopped

2 garlic cloves, crushed

1 cup canned tomatoes, drained, diced

5 potatoes, peeled and cut into 1/4 inch cubes

1/2 cup fresh parsley leaves, finely cut

3 tbsp olive oil

1 tbsp summer savory or oregano

1 tsp paprika

2/3 cup yogurt

1 egg, lightly beaten

salt and freshly ground black pepper

Directions:

Heat the oil in a large frying pan over medium-high heat. Add the ground meat and cook, stirring, using a spoon to break up lumps, for 5 minutes or until it changes color. Transfer to slow cooker.

In the same pan, add the carrot, onion, garlic, parsley, paprika and summer savory and sauté, stirring, for 10 minutes, or until vegetables soften. Transfer to the slow cooker and mix well with the ground meat.

Wash, peel, and dice the potatoes. Stir them into the meat and vegetable mixture. Co/pmbine very well, add 1/2 cup of water, stir again. Cover and cook on high heat for 2 hours.

In a small bowl, mix together the yogurt and egg, pour and spread it evenly over the Moussaka. Cook for an additional 2 hours. Set aside for five minutes and serve with a dollop of yogurt.

Eggplant Moussaka

Serves 6

Ingredients:

1 1/2 lbs ground beef

3 eggplants, peeled and cut into 1/2 inch thick rounds

1 large onion, chopped

1/2 tsp ground cinnamon

1/4 tsp ground coriander

1/2 cup canned tomatoes, undrained, chopped

1/2 cup parsley leaves, finely chopped

4 tbsp olive oil

1 tsp sugar

1 tsp salt

2/3 cup yogurt

1 egg, beaten

1 cup Parmesan cheese

salt and black pepper, to taste

Directions:

Place eggplant rounds on a tray and sprinkle with plenty of salt. Let sit for 30 minutes, then rinse with cold water. Squeeze out excess water and pat dry.

Heat oil in a frying pan over medium high heat. Cook eggplant, in batches, for 3 to 4 minutes each side, or until golden. Transfer to a plate.

In the same pan sauté onion, stirring, for 3 to 4 minutes, or until softened. Add spice and sauté for one more minute until fragrant. Add ground beef, garlic, sugar and tomatoes. Stir and cook until the meat is no longer pink.

Arrange half the eggplant slices in a slow cooker. Cover with meat mixture and arrange remaining eggplant. Cover and cook on high heat for 2 hours.

In a small bowl mix together the yogurt, egg, and Parmesan cheese, pour and spread it evenly over the Moussaka. Bake for an additional 2 hours. Set aside for five minutes and serve.

Zucchini Moussaka

Serves 4

Ingredients:

1 lb ground beef

5 zucchinis, peeled and sliced

1/3 cup rice

3-4 garlic cloves, sliced

1 large onion, chopped

1/2 cup canned tomatoes

1/2 cup fresh dill, finely cut

2/3 cup yogurt

1 egg, lightly beaten

4 tbsp olive oil

1 tsp paprika

salt and black pepper, to taste

Directions:

Sauté the onions and garlic for a minute or two, stirring. Add the ground beef and cook it for 10 minutes until it is no longer pink. Add tomatoes, paprika, rice and dill and stir.

Arrange half the zucchini slices in a slow cooker. Spread ground beef mixture over them. Arrange the remaining zucchinis on top. Cover and cook on high for 2 hours.

In a small bowl, mix together the yogurt and egg, pour and spread it evenly over the Zucchini Moussaka. Bake for an additional 1 hour. Set aside for five minutes and serve.

Crock Pot Lasagna

Serves 8

Ingredients:

1 lb lean ground beef

10 oz pancetta or bacon, cut into 1/4-inch pieces

1 small onion, finely chopped

1 carrot, chopped

1 celery rib, chopped

3 garlic cloves, crushed

1/2 cup dry white wine

1/2 cup chicken broth

2 cans tomatoes, diced and undrained

3 tbsp tomato paste

1 tbsp dried basil

1/3 cup parsley

1/2 tsp ground black pepper

1/4 tsp salt

1 tsp paprika

2 cups mozzarella cheese, shredded

1 cup Parmesan cheese, shredded

12 no-boil lasagna noodles

Directions:

ground meat turns brown. Bring to a simmer and cook, uncovered, until liquid is nearly evaporated. Stir in wine and broth and continue simmering until liquid evaporates. Add in paprika, tomatoes, tomato paste, parsley, black pepper and salt.

Combine mozzarella and Parmesan cheese in a medium bowl.

Spread one-third of the meat sauce over the bottom of a slow cooker. Cover with one-fourth of the cheese mixture. Top with 4 noodles, broken into pieces to fit. Repeat layering meat sauce, cheese mixture, and noodles two more times.

Cover and cook on low heat setting 4-6 hours or until noodles are tender. Set aside for 10 minutes and serve.

Beef and Spinach Lasagna

Serves 8-10

Ingredients:

1 lb lean ground beef

10 oz frozen spinach, thawed

1 small onion, chopped

1 can tomatoes, diced and undrained

4 garlic cloves, crushed

1 tsp dried basil

1 tsp dried oregano

2 cups ricotta cheese

2 cups mozzarella cheese, shredded

12 no-cook lasagna noodles

Directions:

In a large skillet, sauté onion for a few minutes. Add beef and cook over medium heat until meat is no longer pink. Add in the tomatoes, garlic, basil and oregano. Simmer for 10 minutes. In a large bowl, combine the thawed spinach with half the ricotta and mozzarella cheese.

Spread one-third of the meat sauce over the bottom of slow cooker. Sprinkle with one-fourth of the spinach-cheese mixture. Top with noodles broken to fit. Repeat layering meat sauce, spinach mixture, and noodles two more times.

Cover and cook on low for 4-6 hours. Let stand for at least 10 minutes before serving.

Mediterranean Bolognaise

Serves 6

Ingredients:

1 lb ground lean beef

1 onion, chopped

2 garlic cloves, finely chopped

2 tbsp tomato paste

1 can tomatoes, diced, undrained

1/4 cup dry white or red wine

1/3 cup dried tomatoes, chopped

1/4 cup black olives, pitted, halved

1/4 cup chopped fresh basil leaves

1 tsp dried oregano

17 oz spaghetti

Parmesan cheese, to serve

Directions:

In a slow cooker, add ground beef, onion, garlic, tomato paste, tomatoes, wine, dried tomatoes, olives, basil and oregano. Season with salt and pepper.

Cover and cook until the vegetables are tender and the meat is cooked through, on low for 6-7 hours or on high for 4-5 hours.

Prepare spaghetti as described on package directions. Wash, drain and divide them between bowls. Top with sauce and sprinkle with Parmesan cheese and fresh basil leaves.

Sausage and Eggplant Stew

Serves: 4

Ingredients:

2 eggplants, peeled and diced

1 onion, chopped

2-3 garlic cloves, crushed

2 lbs Italian sausages, cut into chunks

8 oz can tomatoes, undrained, diced

1 tbsp paprika

1 tsp cumin

3 tbsp olive oil

salt and pepper, to taste

1/2 cup fresh basil leaves, finely cut

Directions:

Heat olive oil in a large deep frying pan and brown sausages on all sides, about 6 minutes total. Add in onion and garlic, paprika, cumin and cinnamon, and cook for 2-3 minutes more, stirring. Transfer to slow cooker.

Add in eggplant and tomatoes and stir to combine. Cover and cook on low for 6-7 hours on high for 4 hours. Season with salt and pepper, stir in basil and serve.

Turkey Sausage and Lentil One-pot

Serves 4

Ingredients:

1 lb lean smoked turkey sausage, cut into 1-inch slices

1 big onion, chopped

2 garlic cloves, crushed

1 red pepper, sliced

1 cup green lentils, rinsed

1 cup vegetable broth

1 tbsp dried mint

1/2 cup finely cut parsley, to serve

Directions:

Spray the slow cooker with non stick spray.

Place sausages, onions, garlic and red pepper in slow cooker. Add in lentils, vegetable broth and mint.

Cover and cook on low for 6-7 hours. Serve sprinkled with fresh parsley.

Slow Cooked Pot Roast

Serves 4

Ingredients:

2 lb pot roast

2 garlic cloves, crushed

1 onion, finely cut

1 tsp paprika

1 tsp summer savory

1/2 tsp cumin

4 tbsp tomato paste

1 cup chicken broth

salt and black pepper, to taste

Directions:

Spray the slow cooker with non stick spray.

Sprinkle salt and black pepper over the roast and place in the slow cooker.

In a bowl, combine the tomato paste, chicken broth, garlic, onions, paprika, savory and cumin. Spread this mixture over the meat.

Cover and cook on low 8-10 hours.

Mediterranean Pork Stew

Serves 4

Ingredients:

1 1/2 lb pork loin, cut into cubes

1 large onion, chopped

1 cup white button mushrooms, cut

2 garlic cloves, finely chopped

1 green pepper, deseeded and cut into strips

1 small eggplant, peeled and diced

1 zucchini, peeled and diced

2 tomatoes, chopped

½ cup chicken broth

1 tsp summer savory

1 tbsp paprika

salt and black pepper, to taste

Directions:

Spray the slow cooker with non stick spray.

Place all ingredients in slow cooker. Cover and cook on low setting for 7-9 hours. Serve with mashed potatoes or rice pilaf.

Moroccan Pork Stew

Serves 4

Ingredients:

2 lbs pork shoulder roast

1 onion, chopped

2 garlic cloves, finely chopped

1 can chickpeas, drained

1 can diced tomatoes

2 cups butternut squash, cubed

1 cup chicken broth

1 tsp ground ginger

1 tsp cumin

1 tsp cinnamon

2 tbsp paprika

salt and black pepper, to taste

Directions:

Combine paprika, ginger, cumin, cinnamon, salt and black pepper in a small dish. Rub pork shoulder roast with spice mixture, coating well. Add squash, chickpeas, tomatoes and broth to bottom of slow cooker. Place roast on top.

Cover and cook on high for 4 hours or until pork roast falls apart easily. Remove roast to a plate or cutting board, shred meat using two forks, and add back to crock pot.

Pork Roast and Cabbage

Serves 4

Ingredients:

2 cups cooked pork roast, chopped

1/2 head cabbage

1/2 onion, chopped

1 lemon, juice only

1 tomato, diced

1/2 cup chicken broth

1 tsp paprika

1/2 tsp cumin

salt and black pepper, to taste

Directions:

Spray the slow cooker with non stick spray.

Combine all ingredients in slow cooker. Cover and cook on low for 4-5 hours.

Orange Pork Chops

Serves 4

Ingredients:

4 pork chops, about 4 oz each

1 onion, thinly sliced

4 garlic cloves, crushed

3 tbsp olive oil

1/4 tsp cumin

1/2 tsp dried oregano

1 tsp black pepper

1 tbsp raw honey

1 cup orange juice

Directions:

Spray the slow cooker with non stick spray.

Crush the garlic, oregano, black pepper and cumin together into a paste. Rub each chop with the garlic paste and arrange them in slow cooker.

Dilute one tablespoon of honey into the orange juice and pour it over the chops. Add in onions.

Cover and cook for 7-9 hours on low setting.

Juicy Pork Chops

Serves 4

Ingredients:

4-5 pork chops, about 4 oz each

4 garlic cloves, crushed

1 tbsp honey

3 tbsp olive oil

1 tbsp vinegar

1/2 cup white wine

1 tbsp soy sauce

1 tbsp ketchup

1/2 tsp dried sage

1 tsp black pepper

1/2 tsp salt

Directions:

Spray the slow cooker with non stick spray.

In a cup, combine all liquid ingredients and stir until very well mixed. Crush the garlic, sage, black pepper and salt together into a paste. Rub each chop with the garlic paste and arrange them in slow cooker.

Pour the liquid mix over the chops. Cover and cook for 7-9 on low.

Pork and Mushroom Crock Pot

Serves 4

Ingredients:

2 lbs pork tenderloin, sliced

2 cups chopped white button mushrooms

1 can cream of mushroom soup

½ cup sour cream

4 tbsp chopped taragon

1/2 tsp black pepper

1/2 tsp salt

Directions:

Spray the slow cooker with non stick spray.

Combine all ingredients into the slow cooker. Cover, and cook on low for 7-9 hours.

Eggplant and Chickpea Stew

Serves: 4

Ingredients:

2-3 eggplants, peeled and diced

1 onion, chopped

2-3 garlic cloves, crushed

8 oz can chickpeas, drained

8 oz can tomatoes, undrained, diced

1 tbsp paprika

1/2 tsp cinnamon

1 tsp cumin

3 tbsp olive oil

salt and pepper, to taste

Directions:

Spray the slow cooker with non stick spray.

Heat olive oil in a large deep frying pan and sauté the onion and crushed garlic for 1-2 minutes, stirring. Add in paprika, cumin and cinnamon. Transfer to slow cooker.

Add in eggplant, tomatoes and chickpeas. Cover and cook on low for 6-7 hours or about 4 hours on high.

Eggplant and Tomato Crock Pot

Serves: 4

Ingredients:

2 eggplants, peeled and diced

1 large onion, chopped

2 carrots, chopped

1 celery rib, chopped

2-3 garlic cloves, crushed

1 can garbanzo beans, rinsed and drained

8 oz can tomatoes, undrained, diced

1 tbsp paprika

2 bay leaves

1 tsp dried basil

salt and pepper, to taste

Directions:

Spray the crock pot with non stick spray.

Combine all ingredients in crock pot.

Cover and cook on low for 6-7 hours or about 4 hours on high. Discard bay leaves before serving.

Slow Cooker Mediterranean Stew

Serves: 6

Ingredients:

1 butternut squash, peeled, seeded, and cubed

2 tomatoes, diced

2 carrots, chopped

1 onion, finely chopped

1 zucchini, peeled and diced

1 eggplant, peeled and diced

1 celery rib, chopped

1 cup green peas, frozen

1/3 cup raisins

1 can tomato sauce

1 tsp sugar

1 tbsp paprika

1/2 tsp cumin

1/2 tsp tumeric

1 tsp black pepper

1 tsp salt

1/2 cup parsley, finely cut, to serve

Directions:

In a slow cooker, combine butternut squash, eggplant, zucchini, peas, tomato sauce, onion, celery, tomatoes, carrot and raisins. Season with salt and black pepper, add paprika, sugar, cumin and tumeric, and stir to combine.

Cover and cook on low for 6-7 hours or 4 hours on high. Serve sprinkled with parsley.

Rice Stuffed Bell Peppers

Serves: 4-5

Ingredients:

8 bell peppers, cored and seeded

11/2 cups rice

2 onions, chopped

1 tomato, chopped

1/2 cup fresh parsley, chopped

2 cups warm water

3 tbsp olive oil

1 tbsp paprika

salt and pepper, to taste

Directions:

Heat the olive oil and sauté the onions for 2-3 minutes. Add in paprika, rice, diced tomato and season with salt and pepper. Add ½ cup of hot water and cook the rice, stirring, until the water is absorbed.

Stuff each pepper with rice mixture using a spoon. Every pepper should be ¾ full. Arrange the peppers in a slow cooker and top up with the remaining warm water.

Cover and cook for 5-6 hours on low setting.

Bell Peppers Stuffed with Beans

Serves: 5

Ingredients:

10 dried red bell peppers

1 cup dried white beans

1 onion, finely cut

3 cloves garlic, chopped

2 tbsp flour

1 carrot, chopped

1 cup fresh parsley, finely cut

1/2 cup crushed walnuts

1 cup vegetable broth

1 tsp paprika

salt, to taste

Directions:

Put the dried peppers in warm water and leave them for 1 hour.

Cook the beans. Gently sauté onion and carrot and combine with the cooked beans. Add in the finely chopped parsley and walnuts. Stir.

Drain the peppers, then fill them with the bean mixture and arrange in a slow cooker, covering the openings with flour to seal them. Add vegetable broth.

Cover and cook on low setting for 4-5 hours.

Stuffed Grapevine Leaves

Serves: 6

Ingredients:

1.5 oz grapevine leaves, canned

2 cups rice

2 onions, chopped

2-3 cloves garlic, chopped

1/2 cup of currants

1/2 cup fresh parsley, finely cut

1/2 cup fresh dill, finely cut

1 lemon, juice only

1 tsp dried mint

1 tsp salt

1/2 tsp black pepper

6 tbsp olive oil

Directions:

Heat 3 tablespoons of olive oil in a frying pan and sauté the onions and garlic until golden. Add the washed and drained rice, the currants, dill and parsley and sauté, stirring. Add in lemon juice, black pepper, dried mint and salt.

Place a grapevine leaf on a chopping board, with the stalk towards you and the vein side up. Place about 1 teaspoon of the filling in the center of the leaf and towards the bottom edge. Fold the bottom part of the leaf over the filling, then draw the sides in and towards the middle, rolling the leaf up. The vine leaves should be well tucked in, forming a neat parcel. The stuffing should feel compact and evenly distributed.

Arrange the stuffed vine leaves in a slow cooker, packing them tightly together. Pour in some water, to just below the level of the stuffed leaves. Cover and cook on low setting for 5-6 hours. Serve warm or cold.

Stuffed Cabbage Leaves

Serves: 8

Ingredients:

20-30 pickled cabbage leaves

1 onion, finely cut

2 leeks, chopped

1 1/2 cup white rice

1/2 cup currants

1/2 cup almonds, blanched, peeled, and chopped

2 tsp paprika

1 tbsp dried mint

1/2 tsp black pepper

½ cup olive oil

salt, to taste

Directions:

Sauté the onion and leeks in olive oil for about 2-3 minutes. Stir in paprika, black pepper and rice and continue sautéing until the rice is translucent. Remove from heat and add the currants, finely chopped almonds and the peppermint. Add salt only if the cabbage leaves are not too salty.

Place a cabbage leaf on a large plate with the thickest part closest to you. Spoon 1-2 teaspoons of the rice mixture and fold over each edge to create a tight sausage-like parcel. Place in the slow cooker, making two or three layers. Cover with a few cabbage leaves and pour over some boiling water so that the water level remains lower than the top layer of cabbage leaves.

Cover and cook on low setting for 6-8 hours.

Vegetable Quinoa Pilaf

Serves 6

Ingredients:

1 cup quinoa

2 cups vegetable broth

1 red bell pepper, chopped

1 small eggplant, peeled and chopped

1 zucchini, peeled and chopped

2 spring onions, thinly sliced

2 garlic cloves, cut

1 tsp dried oregano

salt and pepper, to taste

1/2 cup shredded Parmesan cheese, to serve

Directions:

In a slow cooker, place quinoa and broth and top with remaining ingredients.

Cover and cook on high for 3-4 hours or on low for 5-6 hours. Fluff with a fork, top with Parmesan cheese and salt and pepper if desired. Serve immediately.

Slow Cooker Breakfasts and Desserts

Caramelized Apple and Quinoa Slow Cooker Breakfast

Serves: 4-5

Ingredients:

6 large apples, peeled and chopped

1/2 cup brown sugar

2 eggs

2 cups milk

a pinch of salt

1/2 cup quinoa, rinsed

1 cup steel cut oats

2 cups water

2 tbsp lemon juice

1 tbsp cinnamon

1/2 tsp vanilla extract

Directions:

Spray the slow cooker with non stick spray.

Layer the apples, brown sugar, salt, cinnamon, vanilla and lemon juice into the greased slow cooker. Do not stir.

In a bowl, whisk the eggs into the milk until smooth. Add the water and whisk again. Add in the oats and quinoa and stir to combine. Pour over the apple mixture.

Cook on low for 6-7 hours or on high for 3 hours.

Banana Bread Oatmeal

Serves: 4-5

Ingredients:

3 bananas, peeled and chopped

2 tbsp brown sugar

1 cup steel cut oats

2 tbsp chia seeds

2 tbsp ground flaxseed

3 tbsp raisins or chopped pitted dates

2 cups milk

2 cups water

1/2 tsp cinnamon

1/2 tsp vanilla extract

Directions:

Spray the slow cooker with non stick spray.

Place all ingredients in a slow cooker, stir, cover and cook on high for 3 hours, stirring occasionally.

Mediterranean Vegetable Omelette

Serves 5-6

Ingredients:

1 small onion, finely cut

1 green bell pepper, chopped

3 tomatoes, cubed

1 garlic clove, crushed

6-7 eggs, beaten

1/2 cup feta cheese, crumbled

4 tbsp milk

1/2 cup finely cut parsley

black pepper, to taste

salt, to taste

Directions:

Spray the slow cooker with non stick spray.

In a bowl, combine eggs, milk, feta, salt and pepper until mixed and well combined. Add onion, garlic, tomatoes, and pepper to the slow cooker and stir in the egg-cheese mixture.

Cover and cook on high for 2 hours. Start checking at 1 hour 30 minutes. Omelette is done when eggs are set. Sprinkle with parsley and serve.

Mediterranean Omelette with Fennel, Olives and Dill

Serves 5-6

Ingredients:

1 small onion, finely cut

2 cups thinly sliced fresh fennel bulb

2 tomatoes, cubed

1/4 cup green olives, pitted and chopped

6-7 eggs, beaten

1/2 cup feta cheese, crumbled

3 tbsp milk

3 tbsp finely cut dill

black pepper, to taste

salt, to taste

Directions:

Spray the slow cooker with non stick spray.

In a bowl, combine eggs, milk, feta, dill, salt and pepper until mixed and well combined.

Add onion, tomatoes, fennel and olives to the slow cooker and stir in the egg-cheese mixture.

Cover and cook on high for 2 hours. Check at 1 hour 30 minutes if the eggs are set.

Slow Cooker Omelette with Spinach, Roasted Pepper and Feta

Serves 5-6

Ingredients:

2-3 green onions, finely chopped

5 oz baby spinach

3 roasted red peppers, diced

8 eggs, beaten

1/2 cup feta cheese, crumbled

3 tbsp milk

1 tbsp finely cut dill

black pepper, to taste

salt, to taste

Directions:

In a skillet, saute the spinach in olive oil for 2-3 minutes or until it wilts.

Spray the slow cooker with non stick spray.

In a bowl, combine the eggs, milk, feta, dill, salt and pepper until mixed and well combined.

Add the spinach, green onions and roasted pepper to the slow cooker and stir in the egg-cheese mixture.

Cover and cook on high for 2-3 hours. Check at 2 hours if the eggs are set.

Slow Cooker Cinnamon Apples

Serves 4

Ingredients:

8 medium sized apples, peeled, cut into eighths

1/3 cup walnuts, chopped

3/4 cup brown sugar

3 tbsp maple syrup

3 tbsp raisins

4-5 dried apricots, chopped

2 tsp cinnamon

2 oz melted butter

2 tbsp lemon juice

3 tbsp water

Directions:

Spray the slow cooker with non stick spray.

In slow cooker, toss apples and lemon juice to coat. Add in brown sugar, walnuts, maple syrup, raisins, apricots, melted butter and cinnamon. Stir to combine.

Cover and cook on low for 4-5 hours.

Slow Cooker Rice Pudding

Serves 4

Ingredients:

1/2 cup short-grain white rice

6 tbsp sugar

1-1/4 cups 2% milk

2 eggs, lightly beaten

1 cinnamon stick

1 strip lemon zest

pistachios, to serve

Directions:

In a slow cooker, combine the first six ingredients. Cover and cook on low for 2 hours. Stir, cover and cook 1-2 hours longer or until rice is tender. When ready discard cinnamon stick and lemon zest. Serve sprinkled with pistachios.

FREE BONUS RECIPES: 10 Ridiculously Easy Jam and Jelly Recipes Anyone Can Make

A Different Strawberry Jam

Makes 6-7 11 oz jars

Ingredients:

4 lb fresh small strawberries (stemmed and cleaned)

5 cups sugar

1 cup water

2 tbsp lemon juice or 1 tsp citric acid

Directions:

Mix water and sugar and bring to the boil. Simmer sugar syrup for 5-6 minutes then slowly drop in the cleaned strawberries. Stir and bring to the boil again. Lower heat and simmer, stirring and skimming any foam off the top once or twice.

Drop a small amount of the jam on a plate and wait a minute to see if it has thickened. If it has gelled enough, turn off the heat. If not, keep boiling and test every 5 minutes until ready. Two or three minutes before you remove the jam from the heat, add lemon juice or citric acid and stir well.

Ladle the hot jam in the jars until 1/8-inch from the top. Place the lid on top and flip the jar upside down. Continue until all of the jars are filled and upside down. Allow the jam to cool completely before turning right-side up. Press on the lid to check and see if it has sealed. If one of the jars lids doesn't pop up- the jar is not sealed–store it in a refrigerator.

Raspberry Jam

Makes 4-5 11 oz jars

Ingredients:

4 cups raspberries

4 cups sugar

1 tsp vanilla extract

1/2 tsp citric acid

Directions:

Gently wash and drain the raspberries. Lightly crush them with a potato masher, food mill or a food processor. Do not puree, it is better to have bits of fruit.

Sieve half of the raspberry pulp to remove some of the seeds. Combine sugar and raspberries in a wide, thick-bottomed pot and bring mixture to a full rolling boil, stirring constantly. Skim any scum or foam that rises to the surface. Boil until the jam sets.

Test by putting a small drop on a cold plate – if the jam is set, it will wrinkle when given a small poke with your finger. Add citric acid, vanilla, and stir. Simmer for 2-3 minutes more, then ladle into hot jars. Flip upside down or process 10 minutes in boiling water.

Raspberry-Peach Jam

Makes 4-5 11 oz jars

Ingredients:

2 lb peaches

1 1/2 cup raspberries

4 cups sugar

1 tsp citric acid

Directions:

Wash and slice the peaches. Clean the raspberries and combine them with the peaches is a wide, heavy-bottomed saucepan. Cover with sugar and set aside for a few hours or overnight. Bring the fruit and sugar to a boil over medium heat, stirring occasionally. Remove any foam that rises to the surface.

Boil until the jam sets. Add citric acid and stir. Simmer for 2-3 minutes more, then ladle into hot jars. Flip upside down or process 10 minutes in boiling water.

Blueberry Jam

Makes 4-5 11 oz jars

Ingredients:

4 cups granulated sugar

3 cups blueberries (frozen and thawed or fresh)

3/4 cup honey

2 tbsp lemon juice

1 tsp lemon zest

Directions:

Gently wash and drain the blueberries. Lightly crush them with a potato masher, food mill or a food processor. Add the honey, lemon juice, and lemon zest, then bring to a boil over medium-high heat. Boils for 10-15 minutes, stirring from time to time. Boil until the jam sets.

Test by putting a small drop on a cold plate – if the jam is set, it will wrinkle when given a small poke with your finger. Skim off any foam, then ladle the jam into jars. Seal, flip upside down or process for 10 minutes in boiling water.

Triple Berry Jam

Makes 4-5 11 oz jars

Ingredients:

1 cup strawberries

1 cup raspberries

2 cups blueberries

4 cups sugar

1 tsp citric acid

Directions:

Mix berries and add sugar. Set aside for a few hours or overnight. Bring the fruit and sugar to the boil over medium heat, stirring frequently. Remove any foam that rises to the surface. Boil until the jam sets. Add citric acid, salt and stir.

Simmer for 2-3 minutes more, then ladle into hot jars. Flip upside down or process 10 minutes in boiling water.

Red Currant Jelly

Makes 6-7 11 oz jars

Ingredients:

2 lb fresh red currants

1/2 cup water

3 cups sugar

1 tsp citric acid

Directions:

Place the currants into a large pot, and crush with a potato masher or berry crusher. Add in water, and bring to a boil. Simmer for 10 minutes.

Strain the fruit through a jelly or cheese cloth and measure out 4 cups of the juice. Pour the juice into a large saucepan, and stir in the sugar. Bring to full rolling boil, then simmer for 20-30 minutes, removing any foam that may rise to the surface. When the jelly sets, ladle in hot jars, flip upside down or process in boiling water for 10 minutes.

White Cherry Jam

Makes 3-4 11 oz jars

Ingredients:

2 lb cherries

3 cups sugar

2 cups water

1 tsp citric acid

Directions:

Wash and stone cherries. Combine water and sugar and bring to the boil. Boil for 5-6 minutes then remove from heat and add cherries. Bring to a rolling boil and cook until set. Add citric acid, stir and boil 1-2 minutes more.

Ladle in hot jars, flip upside down or process in boiling water for 10 minutes.

Cherry Jam

Makes 3-4 11 oz jars

Ingredients:

2 lb fresh cherries, pitted, halved

4 cups sugar

1/2 cup lemon juice

Directions:

Place the cherries in a large saucepan. Add sugar and set aside for an hour. Add the lemon juice and place over low heat. Cook, stirring occasionally, for 10 minutes or until sugar dissolves. Increase heat to high and bring to a rolling boil.

Cook for 5-6 minutes or until jam is set. Remove from heat and ladle hot jam into jars, seal and flip upside down.

Oven Baked Ripe Figs Jam

Makes 3-4 11 oz jars

Ingredients:

2 lb ripe figs

2 cups sugar

1 ½ cups water

2 tbsp lemon juice

Directions:

Arrange the figs in a Dutch oven, if they are very big, cut them in halves. Add sugar and water and stir well. Bake at 350 F for about one and a half hours. Do not stir.

You can check the readiness by dropping a drop of the syrup in a cup of cold water – if it falls to the bottom without dissolving, the jam is ready. If the drop dissolves before falling, you can bake it a little longer. Take out of the oven, add lemon juice and ladle in the warm jars. Place the lids on top and flip the jars upside down. Allow the jam to cool completely before turning right-side up.

If you want to process the jams - place them into a large pot, cover the jars with water by at least 2 inches and bring to a boil. Boil for 10 minutes, remove the jars and sit to cool.

Quince Jam

Makes 5-6 11 oz jars

Ingredients:

4 lb quinces

5 cups sugar

2 cups water

1 tsp lemon zest

3 tbsp lemon juice

Directions:

Combine water and sugar in a deep, thick-bottomed saucepan and bring it to the boil. Simmer, stirring until the sugar has completely dissolved.

Rinse the quinces, cut in half, and discard the cores. Grate the quinces, using a cheese grater or a blender to make it faster. Quince flesh tends to darken very quickly, so it is good to do this as fast as possible.

Add the grated quinces to the sugar syrup and cook uncovered, stirring occasionally until the jam turns pink and thickens to desired consistency, about 40 minutes. Drop a small amount of the jam on a plate and wait a minute to see if it has thickened. If it has gelled enough, turn off the heat. If not, keep boiling and test every 2-3 minutes until ready.

Two or three minutes before you remove the jam from the heat, add lemon juice and lemon zest and stir well.

Ladle in hot, sterilized jars and flip upside down.

About the Author

Vesela lives in Bulgaria with her family of six (including the Jack Russell Terrier). Her passion is going green in everyday life and she loves to prepare homemade cosmetic and beauty products for all her family and friends.

Vesela has been publishing her cookbooks for over a year now. If you want to see other healthy family recipes that she has published, together with some natural beauty books, you can check out her Author Page on Amazon.

Printed in Great Britain
by Amazon

47286337R00078